better together*

*This book is best read together, grownup and kid.

a kids book about™

COVID-19

*coronavirus disease 2019

by Malia Jones

a kids book about™

Printed in the United States of America

Library of Congress cataloging available.

A Kids Book About books are exclusively available
online at *www.akidsbookabout.com*

To share your stories, ask questions, or inquire about
bulk purchases (schools, libraries, and nonprofits),
please use the following email address:

hello@akidsbookabout.com

www.akidsbookabout.com

ISBN: 978-1-951253-31-8

For my boys Owen and Desmond,
the best teachers I've ever had.

Intro

The world is facing an unprecedented public health crisis. I study epidemics, and even though I mostly understand what's happening, I have felt uncertain and vulnerable over these last few months too. A lot of adults are feeling uncertain and afraid.

As a parent (and a scientist), I know kids can tell when grownups feel afraid, worried, lonely, angry, or sad. I want to teach my kids that it's okay to have feelings and talk about them. I want them to know that we've got each other, and that it feels better to have an honest conversation than to try to hide our feelings.

You might not be an epidemiologist, but you are definitely the expert your kids need to lead a conversation. They're ready to talk about it. I wrote this book to give you a starting point for that conversation.

Hi, my name is Malia.

And I'm a Social Epidemiologist.*

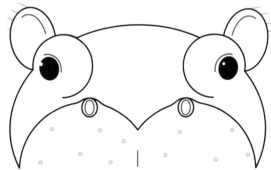

*Not to be confused with a friendly hippopotamus.

That means I'm a scientist who studies

how human diseases spread.

This is my book about a new disease called

COVID-19.

Do you know what that stands for?

It stands for:

coronavirus disease 2019

(because it started in the year 2019).

By now you've definitely already heard about **COVID-19**, or its more common name, **coronavirus**

because
everyone
is talking
about **it**
ALL
the time

......It's a pandemic.* ———

*A pandemic is a disease outbreak that is happening all over the world.

Your school might be closed,
sports might be canceled,
and even the grownups around you
might be a bit scared* or confused.

*It's ok to feel scared, even if you're a grownup.

It seems like the entire world is thinking about one thing......

CORON

AVIRUS

So I'm here to tell you what **coronavirus** is (and isn't).

Coronavirus is a new disease.

COVID-19 has never existed
in the entire history of the world.

That means no one has ever had it.

Until 2019.

COVID-19 is caused by a virus.*

*The virus is called SARS-Cov-2, and the disease it causes
is called COVID-19, but a lot of people just call it all coronavirus.

A virus is a very tiny thing

(so tiny you need a microscope to see it)

that can get inside your body
and make lots of copies of itself.

This can make you sick.

You've definitely had a virus before —
they cause things like colds and the flu.

Coronavirus can cause a fever,
cough,
stuffy nose,
fatigue,
or a headache.

FUN FACT

It can even make you lose your sense of smell for a few weeks!

Some people who get it
never even notice they're sick,

and other people just have
a little run-down feeling.

But a few people who get
coronavirus get very sick.

Like really

really

really

really

really
really
really
really
really
really
really
really
really
really
really
really
really
really
really
really
really
really sick.
So sick they have to go to the hospital.

(If they get too sick, they could even die from coronavirus.)

Lucky for you,
kids don't usually get very sick
when they get **coronavirus**

BUT you can still give it to other people.

You might have heard that **coronavirus** is just like the flu.

IT'S NOT!

Here are some ways **coronavirus** isn't like the flu. ────────

IT'S
DIFFERENT

It's not the same
virus as influenza.

IT'S
NEW

Scientists are working on a vaccine*, but it's not ready yet.

And up until 2019, no one ever had this virus before.

*A vaccine is a medicine that keeps you from getting a virus by giving your body instructions on how to fight it later on. Usually vaccines are given as shots.

IT'S SPREADING
FASTER

COVID-19

infects you quickly and is good at getting other people sick.

IT'S MORE
DANGEROUS

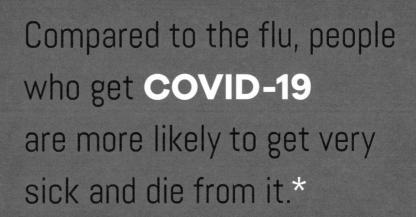

Compared to the flu, people who get **COVID-19** are more likely to get very sick and die from it.*

*The people who get very sick are usually older or already sick with another disease.

There's still a lot we don't know about **coronavirus** because it's so new.

Scientists are learning new things
about it LITERALLY every day!

But one thing we know for sure, is how you get it..........

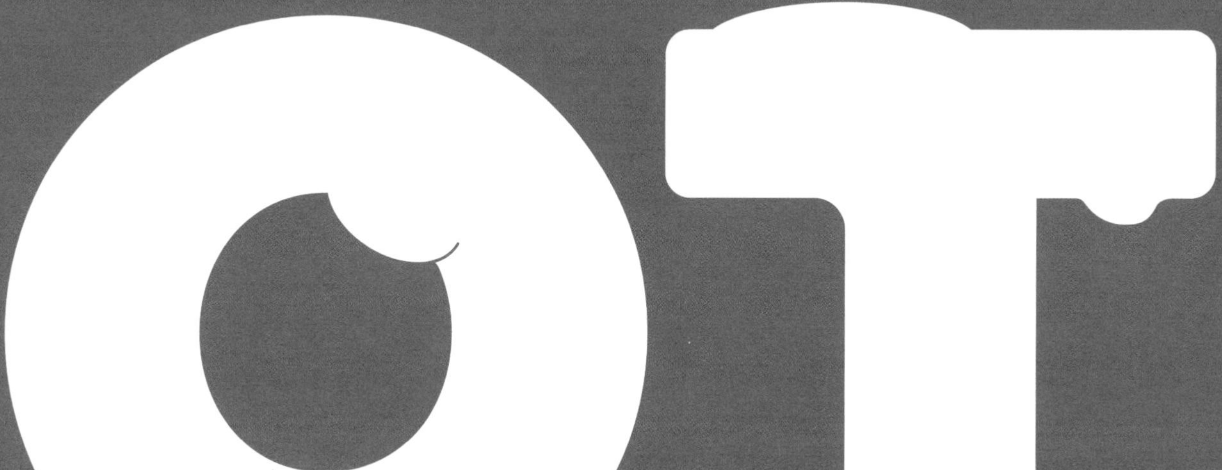
OT

When someone coughs or sneezes,
snot and spit flies out of their mouths and

noses like a massive explosion of...

MS!*

*Germs are tiny little particles that can cause you to get sick.
Viruses are one kind of germ. Bacteria are another kind.

Those germs land on all sorts of things
and stick there, sometimes for a few days.

Door handles, tables, tablets, and pencils.

Even sandwiches.

When you touch something that has
viruses on it, they stick to your hands.
Then if your hand touches your nose
or mouth*, the viruses can get
into your body!

*Viruses are happy in mouths and noses,
 where they can make lots of copies of themselves.

You could even accidentally breathe those bits of snot in if you're close enough to someone.

YES,

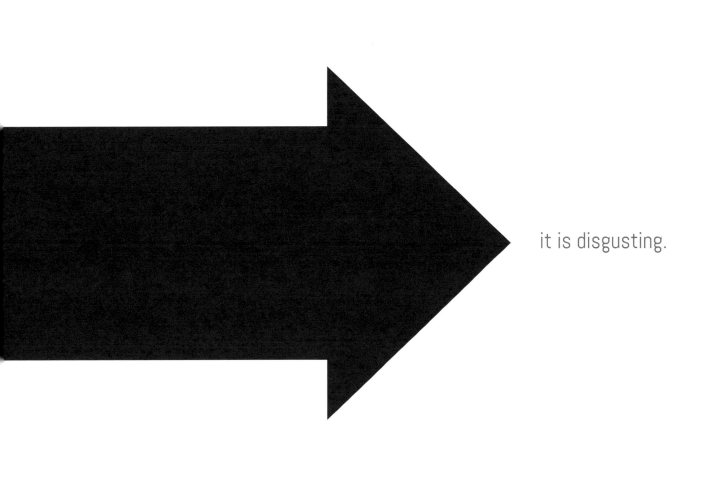

it is disgusting.

Scientists call this "droplet transmission.*"

*We could have just called it snot,
but scientists like to use very specific words.

Droplet transmission is one way viruses get from one person to another. It catches a ride on small drops of spit or snot.

I know this all might seem really scary and
you might want to panic. —
                         / | \

A lot of grownups might want to panic too, and it is a little scary.

It's ok to feel whatever you're feeling.

But here's what **you** can do to help!

WEAR A

to cover your mouth and nose.

Wearing a mask keeps **germs** inside the mask and out of the air around you.

This protects other people from your germs.

DON'T PICK

NO

YOUR

SE

or put your fingers
in your mouth.

Even if your fingers don't look dirty, they could have **viruses** on them!

So try to keep your hands out of your nose and mouth.

If you insist on picking your nose, even after an <u>actual scientist</u> just told you not to, do it with clean hands.

Which brings me to my next point........

WASH YOUR HANDS

...as often as you can. Keeping your hands clean helps a lot!

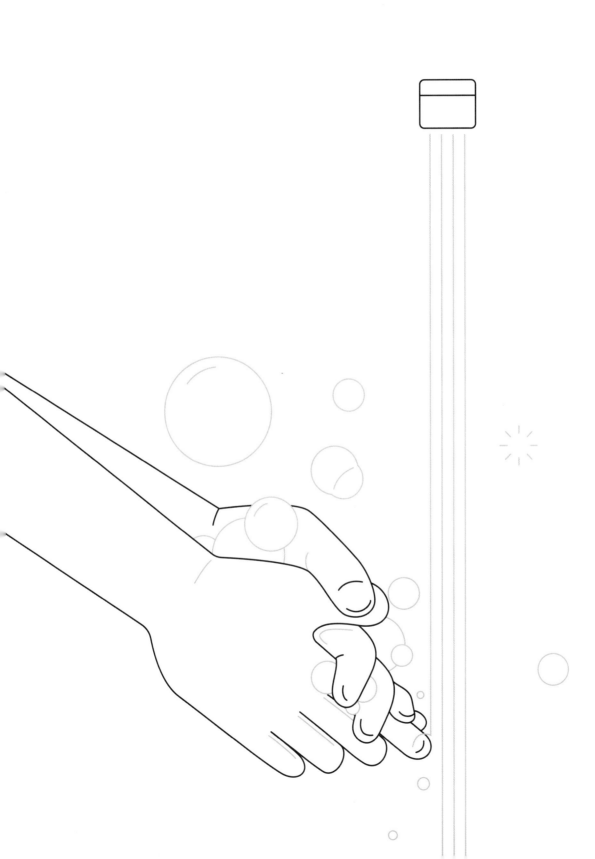

Use soap and water and wash for
20 seconds, or as long as it takes
to sing Baby Shark all the way through.
Or, pick another song you love to sing!

It's especially important to have clean hands when you eat.

If there are too many people getting sick in your town, you might need to... ___

COCOON
for a little while.

Which means that, for a little while, stick close to home and don't spend time near other people.

It's okay to go outside, but don't do it with groups of other kids.

Scientists call this "social distancing.*"

_____ *I told you, scientists love to use big words!

If there are too many people who have **COVID-19** in your area, we all have to go back into our cocoons for a little while to keep us all safer.

Just in case you already have it
(and you don't even know),
we might need you to stay away
from other people who could
get it from you.

Are you worried that you already have it and could give it to your grownups?

It's not your fault if that happens.

It's not your job to figure out who has it.

Scientists are working on that
as fast as they can.

It's your job

to be a kid.

And while you're just being a kid,
you can do a lot for everyone else
by doing simple things
like wearing a mask,
washing your hands,
not picking your nose,
and cocooning for a while.

———————————————→ We need to work TOGETHER.

If we work TOGETHER,

fewer people will get sick and be in danger.

If we work
TOGETHER,

the disease will spread more slowly
and scientists will have more time
to figure out a faster way to test people
for **coronavirus**, the best treatment,
and a vaccine.

It will take everyone's help to stop **COVID-19** in its tracks.

If everyone helps,
we can keep ourselves safer and
keep the people around us safer too.

COVID-19 facts:

→ Widespread, rapid testing is critical to dealing with the COVID-19 pandemic. We need to know who has it in order to prevent further spread of the virus.

→ There are actually lots of different coronaviruses out there and have been for a long time. It's a whole family of viruses. They're called coronaviruses because when you look at them under a microscope, they are shaped like a sun or a corona. This particular coronavirus is brand new to the world.

→ This coronavirus is a genetic cousin to the virus that caused the SARS outbreak in 2003 which affected more than 8,000 people before it was contained successfully.

→ The virus that causes COVID-19 probably came from an ancestor virus that infected some other animal population. Scientists think it might have been a bat, but we don't know for sure.

→ Dogs and cats can get COVID-19 but they very rarely do, and so far, no human that we know of has caught it from their pet

⟶ Soap kills viruses by making them explode.

⟶ We don't know how many people who get COVID-19 will die from it, but we think it's somewhere around 15 in 1000.

⟶ We also don't know how many people will ultimately get COVID-19. But we do know that the slower the pandemic happens, the easier it will be to deal with.

⟶ People from Asia, or with ancestors from Asia, are no more or less likely to get or transmit COVID-19 than anyone else. All humans can get the virus. Older humans are more likely to get seriously ill and need to be cared for in a hospital.

⟶ Scientists are already trying out new treatments, but a vaccine won't be available for a while.

⟶ Scientists who study epidemics are called epidemiologists. Epidemiologists are one part of a science called public health, the study of how groups of people stay healthy. Maybe you can help prevent the next pandemic when you grow up by studying public health!

Outro

Now that you're equipped with all this information, what do you do now? Hopefully you start out by just talking to your kiddo. I am sure they'll have questions and certainly some thoughts of their own. Try to listen as much as you talk. Hear them out.

Then, try these questions:

1. What are you worried about right now?

2. What questions do you still have about coronavirus?

3. What creatures do you know of that use a cocoon for protection?

4. What are you most grateful for today?

find more kids books about

bullying, creativity, racism, divorce, empathy, shame, disabilities, belonging, failure, money, and anxiety.

 **akidsbookabout.com**

share
your read*

*Tell someboady, post a photo,
or give this book away to share
what you care about.